THE
CABINET

Barbara Silberdick Feinberg

Twenty-First Century Books

A Division of Henry Holt and Company
New York

Twenty-First Century Books
A Division of Henry Holt and Company, Inc.
115 West 18th Street
New York, NY 10011

Henry Holt® and colophon are trademarks of
Henry Holt and Company, Inc.
Publishers since 1866

Published in Canada by Fitzhenry & Whiteside Ltd.
195 Allstate Parkway, Markham, Ontario L3R 4T8

Library of Congress Cataloging-in-Publication Data
Feinberg, Barbara Silberdick.
The cabinet / Barbara Silberdick Feinberg. — 1st ed.
p.   cm. — (Inside government)
Summary: Provides a historical perspective for the development
of the cabinet with heads of executive departments of government
as advisers to the president.
Includes bibliographical references and index.
1. Cabinet officers—United States—Juvenile literature. [1. Cabinet officers.]
I. Title. II. Series.

JK611.F38	1995
353.04—dc20	94–41760
	CIP
	AC

ISBN 0–8050–3421–8
First Edition—1995

Designed by Kelly Soong

Printed in Mexico
All first editions printed on acid-free paper ∞.
10 9 8 7 6 5 4 3 2 1

Photo Credits
Cover images courtesy of: U.S. Government Printing Office (flag), U.S.
Department of Education, U.S. Department of Health & Human Services, U.S.
Department of the Treasury, U.S. Department of Labor, U.S. Department of
Agriculture

p. 9, 15, 44, 47: The Bettmann Archive; p. 13, 21: North Wind Picture Archives;
p. 18, 25, 30, 49: UPI/Bettmann; p. 19, 31: AP/Wide World Photos; p. 35: The
White House; p. 40: National Park Service/Dwight D. Eisenhower Library

☆

*To my aunt Anna Scheldon Bunshaft, an
energetic, self-reliant, caring woman*

☆ ══ ACKNOWLEDGMENTS ══ ☆

I would like to thank the following people for helping me locate some of the information used in this book: Irving Adelman, Assistant Director, Head of Reference, East Meadow Public Library; Marilyn Bunshaft, Community Affairs Officer, East Meadow Public Library; Jeremy R. Feinberg, Columbia University School of Law, Class of 1995; Suzanne Freedman, freelance researcher; and Ryan Johnson and Yolanda Logan, 1993 Cabinet Affairs interns at the White House.

I am also grateful to the following people who encouraged me while I was preparing the manuscript: Doug and Jeremy Feinberg, Gina Cane, Lillian Williams, Naomi Neft, Paula Ruderman, Jeanie Smart, and Susan Zito. They endured my grumbles and moans at times when I had put in too many hours at the word processor, and shared my joy when I found an interesting fact to present to my readers.

☆ *April 1994*

CONTENTS

ONE
INTRODUCING
THE CABINET

The president's cabinet of government advisers is not entirely an American invention. Although it has a distinctive identity, its roots can be traced back to Great Britain. For centuries, British monarchs used to meet with their privy, or private, council to discuss important matters affecting the kingdom. Only a few trusted members of this group were asked to give advice to their sovereign. They gathered in a room hardly bigger than a closet, known as the cabinet. It was located near the monarch's personal chambers. Some of the other privy councillors were jealous and began to ridicule these royal favorites by calling them the cabinet. Gradually, the word gained respect. It came to mean a small group of lawmakers who advised the monarch and actually governed the nation.

Now, under the leadership of a prime minister, the British cabinet presents its program of laws to the rest of the nation's lawmakers for their approval. If important parts of that program are rejected, the cabinet resigns and a new election is held. Cabinet members also put into effect laws that have already been approved. They have this responsibility because they are in charge of individual government departments, organizations that supervise and conduct the nation's foreign relations, agricultural and industrial programs, and so forth.

The heads of government departments are called secretaries. In the past, royal secretaries simply prepared letters and official papers for British monarchs. Their work made them familiar with the state secrets these documents contained. In the sixteenth century, during the reign of Queen Elizabeth I, the title secretary began to be given to the official who helped the queen govern, her secretary of state. Over time, when more departments were added to the royal government, their directors were also given the title of secretary.

Americans kept some of the British terminology but set up a much weaker type of cabinet that advises but does not govern. This happened because the two nations developed different types of elective government. Their leaders, the prime minister and the president, were not given the same powers to carry out their particular duties. The nations' lawmakers had different responsibilities toward the cabinet as well. As a result, the two cabinets share little more than a name.

Like the early British royal councils, the American cabinet only advises the president. What's more, the president does not have to accept its suggestions. He can turn to many other officials for information and advice in order to propose programs to Congress. For example, he may choose to follow recommendations from members of the Council of Economic Advisors, which watches the nation's economic output and employment levels, or members of the Council on Environmental Quality, which monitors efforts to control pollution. He may also discuss matters with his aides on the White House staff, such as the national security advisor, who warns him about threats to the nation from abroad.

The president may also consult private individuals. This is what President Andrew Jackson did. Since members of his cabinet did not get along with one another or with him, he turned to a group of close friends for advice. They soon became known as his Kitchen Cabinet because they gathered in the kitchen to talk about the issues of the day. President Franklin D. Roosevelt often asked for opinions from his "brain trust," a group of scholars and experts he recruited to help him with government problems. As a result, the cabinet is only as powerful as a president chooses to make it. While President Dwight D. Eisenhower

An early American caricature of President Jackson
presumably driving away his appointed cabinet members
in favor of his Kitchen Cabinet.

relied on his cabinet for advice, President John F. Kennedy more or less ignored it.

Like the British, the American cabinet includes the heads of government departments, called secretaries. On the other hand, it also admits officials the British do not have, such as the vice president. He is a permanent member of the cabinet and leads the discussion when the president is not available. In addition, the president may invite other appointed government officers to attend cabinet meetings on a regular basis. For example, Madeleine K. Albright, the United States ambassador to the United Nations, was asked to join President Bill Clinton's cabinet.

Unlike British cabinet members, the heads of government departments in the United States are not permitted to be lawmakers. As a result, they cannot govern. Cabinet members are prevented from serving in Congress while managing a department because that would violate the constitutional principle of separation of powers. This is the division of American government into three distinct parts: the legislature, to make laws; the executive branch, to carry out laws; and the judiciary, to judge laws and make sure they are fair.

The heads of cabinet departments are part of the executive branch of government. They must put into effect laws passed by Congress as well as programs recommended by the president. Of course, cabinet members' loyalties may be tested when the president and Congress do not agree. Cabinet officers may appear before Congress only to ask for funds, answer questions, recommend laws, or explain how they are performing their duties. Unlike British heads of departments, they cannot vote on laws affecting the nation.

This arrangement does not encourage the unity found in other governments where cabinets combine executive and legislative duties. Heads of departments in the United States find it more difficult to do their jobs. They may not always be able to advise the president effectively. Why the American cabinet developed differently from the British becomes clear by looking at the way it began.

TWO
DEVELOPING A PRESIDENTIAL CABINET

It took the British several hundred years to develop cabinet government. The Americans, benefiting from British experience, needed far less time. The beginnings of the presidential cabinet can be traced to the Second Continental Congress (1776–1781), which helped conduct the American War of Independence and managed the common business of the newly formed states. The Congress appointed committees to carry out some of its decisions, including one to handle relations with European nations. These committees were the "grandparents" of today's cabinet departments.

The "parents" of present-day cabinet members were the officials who managed finance, foreign affairs, and war under the nation's first constitution, the Articles of Confederation (1781–1788). They were appointed by the new Congress. The officials did not meet together in a group to discuss problems or to offer their advice to Congress. Instead, they each reported separately to the lawmakers and were responsible to them.

The Articles had created an association of American states and a weak national government. Because the states were independent and took whatever actions they wished, this arrangement could work only if they cooperated with one another. They did not. As a result, Congress could not develop a common money system, raise taxes, govern the people directly, or keep the states from quarreling among themselves over trade. In 1787, as conditions worsened, fifty-five American patriots met in Philadelphia to remedy the defects of the Articles. After much debate, they drew up the Constitution, a written document describing and limiting the powers of a new national government.

One of the subjects they debated was whether to set up a cabinet to advise the president. Alexander Hamilton of New York suggested that a president appoint heads of departments of finance, war, and foreign affairs to meet with him and give him advice. Oliver Ellsworth of Connecticut offered an alternative: an executive council made up of the chief justice, or head of the Supreme Court, the highest court in the nation; the president of the Senate, one of two houses of the new Congress; and the heads of executive departments, including foreign affairs, war, the marine (or navy), and finance. The president would not participate in this council. Gouverneur Morris of New York wanted a council of state to be set up. It would include heads of departments of domestic affairs, commerce and finance, state, war, and the marine. Along with the chief justice, they would meet to help the president manage the nation's business. Benjamin Franklin of Pennsylvania argued that a "council of state would not only be a check on a bad president but be a relief to a good one."

Franklin's view did not prevail. There was no mention of a cabinet in the final draft of the Constitution. It was thought that such an advisory council would be an unnecessary burden on the president. Instead, Article 2, section 2, of the Constitution simply stated that the president may require written opinions from the heads of executive departments. He would appoint them, subject to Senate approval. Because the Constitution had created a government based on separation of powers, Article 1, section 6, forbade these officials from sitting in Congress while serving the president.

As the nation's first president, George Washington started from scratch. He could not look to the past to find out what he should do. The Constitution gave him broad, general guidelines, but it did not spell out in detail how he should carry out his

☆ ═══════ ☆

*An engraving of George Washington's "advisers"—the fore-
runners of the cabinet. From left to right: Henry Knox, secretary
of war; Thomas Jefferson, secretary of state; Edmund Randolph,
attorney general; and Alexander Hamilton, secretary of the treasury.*

responsibilities. Washington more or less had to make up the
rules for himself as he went along. He had to find the best way
to fulfill his constitutional duties. What he chose to do or failed
to do would set an example for all the presidents who came after
him. After a few false starts, he decided to seek advice from a
cabinet.

In 1789, at George Washington's request, Congress set up
three departments: State, War, and the Treasury. The post of attor-

ney general was also created, but there was as yet no department of justice. Members of Congress thought that the heads of the departments would consult with them and be responsible to them—as had been the practice under the Articles of Confederation. That is not exactly what happened.

President George Washington needed advice to govern the new nation. At first, he asked his friends in Congress and the Supreme Court for their opinions on a number of different issues. The senators were very uncomfortable when he met with them to find out how they felt about an Indian treaty. They did not want to become his advisory council. Members of the Court were reluctant to advise him because they thought they would be violating the constitutional principle of separation of powers.

Washington then began to consult with the individual heads of the executive departments. He wrote down questions for them to discuss. Later, they began to meet at the home of Secretary of State Thomas Jefferson, where each official wrote his reply to the president's queries. Eventually, Washington held formal meetings with them. When he was absent from the nation's capital, he even asked Vice President John Adams to preside over the meetings. In this way, George Washington created the presidential cabinet, but he called his group of advisers the "confidential officers of the government." In 1793, James Madison, then a member of Congress, first referred to the advisers as the cabinet, a name they kept.

The cabinet developed almost accidentally. As a group, it only gave advice. It had no constitutional or legal responsibilities. This is probably why it never became a powerful part of the government. Attempts were made to strengthen the cabinet, first by making it responsible to Congress and then by adding to its duties. In 1864 and several times later on, the nation's lawmakers, following the British example, introduced measures to let members of the cabinet take seats in the House of Representatives, one of the two houses of Congress. Congress

☆ ═══════ ☆

*Thomas Francis Bayard, secretary of state from
1885–1889, would have been third in line to succeed
Grover Cleveland as president.*

would have gained information about the presidents' plans and programs, and the cabinet secretaries might have had more influence in government as members of Congress. On the other hand, their loyalty to the president might have been severely tested. The measures never passed. They would have violated the Constitution.

In 1886, Congress gave individual heads of departments an additional responsibility, but even that was unlikely to be used. If both the president and the vice president died or were unable to complete their terms in office, a cabinet member would become president. Starting with the secretary of state, the presidential succession would follow the order in which the departments were created. In 1947, however, a new presidential succession law placed two members of Congress before cabinet secretaries on the list of possible presidential replacements. The change was made because both the president and members of Congress were elected by the people, while the heads of departments were appointed officials.

In 1967, the Twenty-fifth Amendment to the Constitution made these arrangements less likely to be needed. It allowed presidents to name their own vice presidents, should the office of vice president become vacant. It did, however, give the cabinet the duty of deciding whether a president was too ill to remain in office. The cabinet would alert Congress if necessary, so that the vice president could temporarily become acting president. This added responsibility has not done much to strengthen the cabinet. Over the years, however, even though the cabinet as a group has not increased in power, it certainly has increased in size.

THREE

INCREASING THE SIZE
OF THE CABINET

Congress has added new executive departments to the national government and, in some cases, combined or removed old ones. These changes reflect the shifting interests and needs of the American people. Since the United States was founded, the nation has expanded from thirteen states to fifty; from a collection of farming communities to vast industrial cities and their surrounding suburbs; from a population mostly made up of northern Europeans, African slaves, and Native Americans to a diverse society of people who can trace their roots all over the world.

At first, Americans thought of themselves as citizens of their states rather than as members of one nation. They looked to state governments to solve their problems. With the growth of mass communications, such as the telegraph, the telephone, radio, and television, and cross-country transportation, such as intercontinental railroads, planes, and trucking, people grew more aware of their common ties as Americans. In addition, many problems, such as pollution, unemployment, and crime, began to cross state boundaries, and the individual states no longer had the resources to solve them. As a result, the national government became more involved in citizens' daily lives and added more departments to meet citizens' needs.

A typical department is directed by a cabinet secretary. As of 1993, cabinet officers received an annual salary of $148,400, an amount set by Congress. The secretary supervises an undersec-

	Closures of Domesti(
Number of military bases in U.S. as of 1988	49!
Closed by 1988 Commission	-1(
Today's Recommendation	-3|
Total to Date	-4|

☆ ══════ ☆

Secretary of Defense Richard B. Cheney during a news conference at the Pentagon announcing the additional closing of thirty-one major domestic military installations.

retary and a number of assistant secretaries who manage the department's major programs. Other assistants help with the department's hiring and dismissal of employees, budgets, and public relations. Altogether, there are about three million people working in the executive departments and in other government agencies. They are known as the federal bureaucracy.

It is difficult to serve as a head of an executive department. Each secretary must serve three masters. Department heads must negotiate with the president and his budget director over how much money the department can spend and what programs should be carried out. They must appear before Congress to get the funds they need to run their department and explain how the money will be used. Finally, the public must support the department's programs for them to be successful. Imagine the pressure President George H. W. Bush's secretary of defense,

Richard B. Cheney, felt in 1991 when he had to announce the president's plan to close military bases. Members of Congress representing areas with bases and townspeople living near the bases made sure he knew how unhappy they were.

Imagine how disappointed President Ronald W. Reagan's first secretary of education, Terrel H. Bell, must have been when the president proved unwilling to keep his campaign promises to put a number of educational reforms into effect. Bell chose to resign in 1984.

Each department is responsible for a number of government programs. Units within the departments, called bureaus, offices, divisions, administrations, or services, manage the programs. For example, the Department of Commerce's Bureau of

☆ ══════ ☆

Secretary of Education Terrel H. Bell gave a parting evaluation of American schools when he resigned in December 1984.

the Census counts the number of people living in the United States every ten years. The Justice Department's Civil Rights Division makes sure that all minorities are treated fairly, and the Treasury Department's Secret Service guards the president. (A description of the most important department subdivisions is included in the following discussion of individual departments.)

The three oldest departments are State, Treasury, and War, established in 1789. The State Department is responsible for the conduct of relations between the United States and other nations as well as with the United Nations, the organization of the world's countries. The department supervises the Foreign Service, professional diplomats who help American ambassadors abroad, and consuls who help businesspeople and tourists. The State Department also has some stateside duties. It publishes all federal laws, makes sure official government documents are genuine, and affixes the Great Seal of the United States to them. The first secretary of state was Thomas Jefferson, who went on to become the third president of the United States.

The Treasury Department is in charge of the nation's finances. Through the United States Mint in the Bureau of Engraving and Printing, it coins and prints the nation's money. The Internal Revenue Service collects federal taxes from individuals and businesses. The United States Savings Bond Division helps the government borrow money from its citizens by selling bonds to them. The Treasury Department also runs the United States Customs Service, which collects fees for items made abroad for sale or use in the United States. The first secretary of the treasury was Alexander Hamilton, who in 1787 and 1788 was one of the authors of *The Federalist Papers*, a brilliant series of articles urging Americans to approve the Constitution.

Until it was replaced by the Defense Department in 1947, the War Department was responsible for the nation's defense. It called up and trained troops, developed military plans, gathered intelligence about enemy plans, and procured weapons and

*General Henry Knox, the first secretary of war
from 1789 to 1795, poses.*

equipment. The department ran the United States Military Academy at West Point. The Air Corps was part of the United States Army from the early days of military aviation in the second decade of the twentieth century until 1947, when it became an independent service. The first secretary of war was Henry Knox, who had fought in the American Revolution at Bunker Hill and served with Washington at Valley Forge. He encouraged the development of the United States Navy.

The Department of the Navy was created in 1798 when John Adams was president. It set up the United States Marine Corps, supervised the building of a fleet, and recruited and trained sailors. It later ran the United States Naval Academy at Annapolis. The first secretary of the navy was Benjamin Stoddert, who had made a fortune in real estate.

The War and Navy departments were merged into the Defense Department at the urging of President Harry S. Truman in 1947. A defense secretary now coordinates the activities of the secretaries of the army, navy, and air force. The first secretary of defense was James V. Forrestal, formerly secretary of the navy. He had to settle many interservice rivalries.

An attorney general advised George Washington and represented the government in legal matters. There was no Department of Justice to direct until 1870, when Ulysses S. Grant was president. The Department of Justice has many divisions. These include an Antitrust Division to break up large businesses that destroy competition in an industry, and a Criminal Division to prosecute those who break federal laws. The most famous unit in the Department of Justice is the Federal Bureau of Investigation, the nation's law enforcement agency. Also well-known is the Drug Enforcement Administration, the nation's narcotics squad. The Immigration and Naturalization Service is in charge of helping foreigners become citizens and requiring those who entered the United States illegally to leave. Among other activities, the department runs the Bureau of Prisons, which houses federal criminals, and operates the United States Marshals Service. The first attorney general was Edmund J. Randolph of Virginia, who had helped to write the Constitution.

The postmaster general became a member of the cabinet in 1829, during Andrew Jackson's presidency. The Post Office, however, did not become an executive department until 1872, while President Ulysses S. Grant was in office. The postmaster general is in charge of the nation's network of post offices, mail services, and postal savings programs. Postmaster General William T. Barry of Kentucky was the first to attend cabinet meetings. Presidents often rewarded the politicians who directed their campaigns for office by putting them in charge of the Post Office. In 1971, the Post Office was dropped from the cabinet as part of President Richard M. Nixon's efforts to reduce government spending. Congress turned the department into an independent, self-supporting agency, the United States Postal Service, with a postmaster general named by a board of governors, who direct its operations.

In 1849, when Zachary Taylor was president, Congress created the Department of the Interior. It manages the National Park Service, which operates Yellowstone and other national parks and monuments, and the United States Fish and Wildlife Service, which protects many species and their habitats. The Bureau of Indian Affairs has responsibility to help Native Americans living on reservations manage their own affairs. The department also has bureaus for land management and mining. In addition, it runs the United States Geological Survey, which studies rocks to discover changes in the earth's crust. The first secretary of the interior was Thomas Ewing, who had served as treasury secretary under Presidents William H. Harrison and John Tyler.

The Department of Agriculture was organized in 1862, but it was headed by a commissioner until 1889. At that time, President Grover Cleveland appointed the first secretary of agriculture to the cabinet. Among its many divisions are the Rural Electrification Administration, which has brought electric power to remote farming areas, and the Food and Nutrition Service, which supervises school lunch programs for students. The department's Animal and Plant Inspection Service protects the food supply, and the United States Forest Service oversees the conservation of trees on public lands. The Agricultural Research Service and the Soil Conservation Service help farmers get more and better crops from their land. The first secretary of agriculture was Norman J. Colman of New York, who had worked hard to get cabinet status for the department.

In 1903, Congress added the Department of Commerce and Labor to President Theodore Roosevelt's cabinet. In 1913, during President Woodrow Wilson's term of office, it was split into two separate departments. The Department of Commerce helps American businesses through its Economic Development Administration, Minority Business Development Agency, and International Trade Administration. Its Patent and Trademark Office gives inventors exclusive rights over their discoveries for a number of years and keeps businesses from copying the logos or brand names of other companies. The department also runs the National Weather Service, which forecasts weather conditions and warns of hurricanes and tornadoes. The first secretary of commerce was William C. Redfield of New York, who became a spokesman for business interests in the cabinet.

The Department of Labor serves American workers. Its Mine Safety and Health Administration and its Occupational Safety and Health Administration try to make workplaces less dangerous. Its Bureau of Labor-Management Relations and Cooperative Programs seeks to ease differences between workers and employers. To help workers qualify for jobs, the department runs the Employment and Training Administration. There is also a Bureau of Labor Statistics to keep track of the number and kinds of jobs in the nation. The first secretary of labor was William B. Wilson of Pennsylvania, who had helped start the United Mineworkers of America and had served as the chairman of the Labor Committee of the House of Representatives.

In 1953, Congress set up the Department of Health, Education, and Welfare, during the presidency of Dwight D. Eisenhower. Oveta Culp Hobby of Texas headed the department and helped it get started. In 1979, during President Jimmy Carter's term, it was divided into the Department of Health and Human Services and the Department of Education.

The Department of Health and Human Services is con-

*President Carter congratulates Patricia Roberts Harris after she
was sworn in as secretary of health and human services in 1979.*

cerned with the public's well-being. It runs the Centers for
Disease Control, which fights infectious illnesses, and the
Alcohol, Drug Abuse, and Mental Health Administration, which
handles those problems. Its National Institutes of Health con-
ducts research and provides treatment for serious illnesses. The
Food and Drug Administration ensures the purity of foods and
the safety of medicines, while the United States Office of
Consumer Affairs protects buyers from misleading advertising
claims and fraud. There are also administrations on aging and on
developmental disabilities. The department's Family Support
Administration operates a number of programs for needy chil-
dren and their caregivers. Patricia Roberts Harris of
Washington, D.C., the first African-American woman to serve as
an ambassador, became secretary of the department. She had

been transferred from the Department of Housing and Urban Development.

The Department of Education seeks to improve the quality of American education for all citizens and offers aid to needy college students. It has assistant secretaries for Elementary and Secondary Education, Bilingual Education and Minority Languages Affairs, and for Vocational and Adult Education, among others. The first Secretary of Education was Shirley Hufstedler of California, who had to organize approximately 150 programs taken over from other departments.

The Department of Housing and Urban Development was established in 1965, when Lyndon B. Johnson was president. It has assistant secretaries for Fair Housing and Equal Opportunity, Community Planning and Development, and Public and Indian Housing, among others. It offers government mortgages, or loans, to help those who want to buy their own homes. The first secretary of housing and urban development was Robert C. Weaver. He was also the first African-American to become the head of a cabinet department.

The Department of Transportation was included in the cabinet in 1966, also during Lyndon B. Johnson's presidency. It operates the United States Coast Guard, which watches over American shores. To protect travelers, it runs the Federal Aviation Administration, the Federal Railroad Administration, the National Highway Traffic Safety Administration, the Maritime Administration, and the Urban Mass Transportation Administration. The first secretary of the department was Alan S. Boyd of Florida, who had served as undersecretary of transportation in the Department of Commerce.

In 1977, Congress created a Department of Energy to conserve the nation's dwindling sources of power and develop new ones. To carry out these goals, the department has assistant secretaries for nuclear energy, which comes from splitting atoms; fossil energy, which comes from coal and oil; and for conservation and renewable energy, which comes from solar, wind, and water power. There are also offices of Civilian Radioactive Waste Management and Energy Research. President Jimmy Carter appointed the first secretary of the department, James R. Schlesinger of Virginia, who had been a chairman of the Atomic Energy Commission and a former secretary of defense.

In 1989, while George H. W. Bush was president, the Department of Veterans Affairs became part of the cabinet. Replacing the Veterans Administration, this newest department runs the Veterans Benefits Administration, the National Cemetery System, and the Veterans Health Services and Research Administration. It helps former members of the armed forces. The first secretary of veterans affairs was Edward Derwinski of Illinois. He was especially concerned about the plight of Vietnam veterans who became sick as a result of chemicals used to strip Vietnam of plant life.

In the future, as the needs of the nation change, there may be new executive departments added to the cabinet. Perhaps others will be reorganized or removed from the cabinet, too. One thing is certain: the men and women who become heads of the executive departments have important jobs to do. They affect the lives of every American.

FOUR
JOINING THE CABINET

Every four years, after the president is elected, the public anxiously waits to find out who will serve in the new cabinet. Richard M. Nixon was the first president to introduce his cabinet appointees to the public on television. All this concern about the cabinet seems strange because it is not a very powerful part of the government. On the other hand, the American people have every reason to be interested in the selection of individual heads of the executive departments. In addition to advising the president, these officials do have important responsibilities that directly affect the public. They carry out presidential programs and laws passed by Congress. As a result, Americans try to determine each cabinet member's political views so that they will know what changes, if any, to expect. For example, they will want to find out how the president's choice for attorney general feels about civil rights, gun control, and law enforcement.

The appointment process often begins before the president-elect, or victorious presidential candidate, takes the oath of office. Today, newly elected presidents often rely on a transition team to help them choose heads of executive departments. This team, often made up of the president's election campaign managers, consults with the White House officials about to leave office and makes plans for taking over the executive branch. After discussions with the party's political leaders, the team may suggest possible cabinet members to the president-elect or narrow down a list given to them. Team members frequently interview cabinet job applicants and receive reports from the FBI on their backgrounds. Of course, the final choices are up to the president.

The president may use cabinet posts to hold his political party together. Political parties sponsor candidates for public office and help them get elected. Quite often, these organizations are divided into factions, small groups that hold common opinions or represent the interests of a certain section of the country. Some factions may even have wanted another person to become the party's presidential candidate. The president's cabinet appointments may help console them. For example, in the 1870s and 1880s, the Republicans were divided between the reformer "Half-Breeds" and their opponents, the "Stalwarts." When compromise candidate James A. Garfield became president in 1881, he tried to unite the party by naming men from each faction to head executive departments. Stalwart Thomas L. James became postmaster general, while Half-Breed Wayne MacVeagh served as attorney general.

The president may prefer to choose cabinet members who are personally loyal to him, individuals he can trust. This is why President John F. Kennedy insisted on making his brother, Robert F. Kennedy, attorney general in 1961. Some Americans were upset that the president named a close relative to such an important government post. From 1969 to 1972, President Richard M. Nixon's attorney general was John N. Mitchell, his close friend and law partner. In 1989, President George H. W. Bush deliberately picked people who shared his views. He chose department heads who would function as a group and not disagree among themselves. His cabinet contained officials who were all practical, moderate, and unlikely to draw attention to themselves.

The president may also appoint members of the opposition party to the cabinet. This is done to gain the opposition's support

☆ ═══════ ☆

From left to right in the back seat of the car touring the historic Shenandoah Valley in Virginia are President Roosevelt; Secretary of Interior Harold Ickes; and Secretary of Agriculture Henry Wallace.

for any new programs. In one case, in 1933, Democratic president Franklin D. Roosevelt named Republican Harold Ickes to be secretary of the interior. In turn, Ickes rallied many Republican conservationists to Roosevelt's side to preserve the nation's natural resources.

In 1993, President Bill Clinton wanted his cabinet to "look like America," to help unify the nation. His appointments reflected the diversity of the American people and included African-Americans, Hispanics, and women. President Franklin D. Roosevelt named the first woman to serve in the cabinet, Labor Secretary Frances Perkins. The first African-American to direct an executive department was Robert C. Weaver, President Lyndon B. Johnson's secretary of housing and urban development. President Ronald W. Reagan appointed the first Hispanic cabinet member, Secretary of Education Lauro F. Cavazos.

According to the Constitution, two-thirds of the members

of the Senate must approve the president's cabinet choices. After the president submits their names, Senate committees question the appointees to make sure they are qualified to serve. The future secretary of state meets with the Senate Committee on Foreign Relations, the future secretary of agriculture meets with the Senate Committee on Agriculture, Nutrition, and Forestry, and so forth. These Senate committees make recommendations to the full Senate to accept or reject each of the president's choices.

So far, only nine intended cabinet members have been turned down by the Senate. Most recently, in 1989, the Senate Committee on Armed Services advised the Senate to block the appointment of John Tower, President Bush's choice for secretary of defense. Even though Tower had previously headed that committee, its members found him unacceptable for the cabi-

☆ ═══════ ☆

Energy secretary-designate, Hazel O'Leary, testified before the Senate Energy Committee, which was holding hearings on her confirmation after President-elect Clinton had appointed her.

net post because he had at one time been a heavy drinker. The Senate rejected him but soon approved Richard B. Cheney, a former congressman, to head up the Defense Department. President Bill Clinton's first choice for attorney general, Zoe Baird, withdrew after she was questioned by the Senate Committee on the Judiciary. Most committee members thought that her failure to pay taxes on the earnings of illegal immigrants working in her home disqualified her from taking on the nation's top law enforcement post. Janet Reno became the new attorney general instead.

The Constitution is silent on the question of how long heads of departments should stay at their posts. At first, cabinet members did not serve for a specific number of years. Then, in 1866, Congress passed a law permitting heads of executive departments to remain for the entire term of the president who appointed them. Nevertheless, there were many holdovers from one president to the next. From the presidencies of John Adams (1797–1801) to Herbert C. Hoover (1929–1933), 110 heads of departments remained in office for two presidential terms in a row. Of course, many presidents were elected for two terms and did not choose to remove them. Only forty-two cabinet members, however, kept their posts when a president from a different political party took office.

If a president is elected for a second term, cabinet holdovers do not have to be approved by the Senate again. For example, President Woodrow Wilson simply kept his cabinet. When presidents have died in office, their successors have often held on to members of their cabinets. This practice was followed by Calvin Coolidge in 1923, after Warren G. Harding's death; by Harry S. Truman in 1945, after Franklin D. Roosevelt died; and by Lyndon B. Johnson in 1963, after John F. Kennedy's assassination.

Newly elected presidents have also let cabinet members of the outgoing president keep their jobs without seeking Senate approval. In all these instances, the presidents were members of the Republican Party. In 1929, President Herbert C. Hoover retained President Calvin Coolidge's secretary of the treasury, Andrew W. Mellon, without submitting his name to the Senate. He knew that some senators disagreed with Mellon's economic programs and might block his reappointment. In 1989, President George H. W. Bush did not bother to seek Senate approval for his secretary of the treasury, Nicholas F. Brady. Brady had served under President Ronald W. Reagan.

Sometimes, presidents may have to overcome obstacles to get the individuals they want appointed to the cabinet. They may face even greater difficulties working with their cabinets.

FIVE
MEETINGS OF THE CABINET

The president meets with the cabinet in the White House Cabinet Room, built by Theodore Roosevelt in 1902. The room was not used regularly for cabinet meetings until 1934, during Franklin D. Roosevelt's first term in office. Cabinet members now sit in identical chairs around a dark wood table donated by President Richard M. Nixon. On the back of each chair is a brass plate that gives the official's name and the date he or she was approved by the Senate. When cabinet officers leave their jobs, staff members purchase the chairs as gifts for them. In 1993, the chairs given to President George H. W. Bush and his cabinet cost almost $1,700 each.

Getting information about what goes on at current cabinet meetings is very difficult. Cabinet minutes, or written records of what was said, and cabinet agendas, schedules of topics for discussion, are not necessarily made public. Presidents do not have to reveal the contents of their private discussions with advisers, except under special circumstances. Their right to withhold such information is called executive privilege. Nevertheless, in 1978, while Jimmy Carter was president, *The Nation* magazine managed to print selections from the minutes of several of his cabinet meetings. Included was this most appropriate topic: "August 1: The president expressed his concern about recent leaks to the press regarding specific discussions at cabinet meetings. He urged cabinet members and White House staff *not* to characterize to the press what he and others say during the cabinet meetings."

It is easier to learn about past presidents' relations with their cabinets. Retired cabinet officials have occasionally written books about their government service that contain descriptions of cabinet meetings. Also, scholars and reporters have written books and articles that analyze the way presidents deal with their heads of executive departments. Fortunately, presidents sometimes permitted glimpses into the workings of their cabinets while they were still in office. For example, an article published in the May 1993 issue of *Mademoiselle* magazine showed how President Bill Clinton's cabinet meetings are run.

When all the cabinet officials are gathered in the Cabinet Room, the secretary of the cabinet, Christine Varney, comes

☆ ══════ ☆

A full cabinet meeting is a hard working session
for all the participants. This is the official photograph of
President Clinton's cabinet taken in January 1994.

into the Oval Office, where Bill Clinton works. She tells the president that they are ready for him. Then he enters the Cabinet Room, and everyone stands up to show respect for the president. During the meeting, Varney sits behind Clinton and takes notes on what is said. Discussions during the meetings are arranged by topic, not by cabinet department. This encourages every cabinet member to participate whenever he or she wishes.

President Bill Clinton allows photographers to take pictures of cabinet meetings. All discussion stops, however, when they are led in, and continues only after they leave. When the time set aside for the meeting is up, presidential aide Andrew Friendly arrives to remind the president to move on to his other duties. President Clinton brings the meeting to an end, stands up, and leaves the room. The cabinet members stand when he does, but they leave by a different door.

How often cabinet meetings are held depends very much on the needs and wishes of the president. Between 1845 and 1849, when James K. Polk was president, he set the record by holding 400 cabinet meetings. Despite this, he did not think the cabinet was very important. Other presidents, such as Andrew Jackson in the 1830s, John F. Kennedy in the 1960s, and Richard M. Nixon in the 1970s, held very few cabinet meetings. They usually chose not to rely on their cabinets for advice. Over the last twenty or so years, cabinets have met weekly.

Presidents tend to see heads of departments more frequently in small groups. They may be said to have an "inner cabinet" and an "outer cabinet." Members of the inner cabinet typically include the secretaries of state, defense, and the treasury as well as the attorney general. Presidents seek advice from these officials for two reasons. First, they are generally individuals the president knows and trusts. Often they have served together in other government posts. Second, their departments are very important in planning and carrying out presidential programs. Presidents John F. Kennedy and Lyndon B. Johnson were among the many presidents who met frequently with their inner cabinets instead of holding many full cabinet meetings.

During wartime, presidents have often consulted with their inner cabinets, along with other officials, and have appointed them to advisory groups. Sometimes, these groups have even received official status. In 1916, on the eve of America's entry into World War I, President Woodrow Wilson set up a Council of National Defense to advise him. It included the secretaries of war, the navy, interior, agriculture, commerce, and labor. After the United States became involved in the conflict, the war was not discussed at full cabinet meetings. President Harry S. Truman did not ask for his cabinet's advice when the Korean War broke out in 1950. Instead, he relied on an informal group made up of the secretaries of state and defense, military advisers, and his closest White House aides. In 1962, once Soviet missiles were discovered in Cuba, President John F. Kennedy created the Executive Committee to help him make important decisions about ridding the island of this threat to American security. Its members included the secretaries of state, defense, and the treasury, the attorney general, and other government officials.

The outer cabinet is concerned with matters taking place mostly within the United States. Its members are the secretaries of agriculture, the interior, labor, commerce, among others. Quite often, presidents appoint individuals from different races, religions, and geographical areas to these posts. They are not necessarily friends of the president or people he has worked with in the past. Presidents usually treat members of their outer cabinets as spokespeople, either for certain economic groups, such as farmers and workers, or for causes, such as endangered species and automobile safety. The secretaries are often more committed to these groups and causes than to the president. For example, President Nixon's first secretary of the interior, Walter J. Hickel, was a strong advocate of conservation and the needs of young people, concerns the president did not share.

Presidents have used cabinet meetings for many different purposes. Some, like Harry S. Truman, have followed George Washington's example and sought advice. In his early years as president, Truman even asked the cabinet to vote on some important matters. President Gerald R. Ford in the 1970s also consulted his cabinet frequently and let the members make decisions on several occasions.

Other presidents gave their cabinets even greater responsibility for governing. Among them were Ulysses S. Grant in the 1870s and Warren G. Harding and Calvin Coolidge in the 1920s. These weak presidents failed to take charge of the government or oversee what department heads were doing. In the 1950s, President Dwight D. Eisenhower also delegated much responsibility to his cabinet officers, but he made sure they would carry out his wishes.

No other twentieth-century president did as much as Eisenhower to make the cabinet an important part of the government. He expanded its membership to include some of his White House advisers and the United States ambassador to the United Nations. Like Grant, Harding, and Coolidge, he expected his heads of departments to run the day-to-day business of government. On the other hand, he used cabinet meetings to keep himself informed about what they were doing, to settle differences among them, and to point out what he wanted them to do. Department heads had to make sure that every cabinet decision was carried out.

In order to make full use of his cabinet, Eisenhower set up the Office of Secretary to the Cabinet and a staff. The secretary coordinated cabinet business while the cabinet staff circulated reports written by the departments. Requiring the heads of departments to prepare and read the reports before each cabinet meeting ensured that important matters would be taken up for discussion. After Eisenhower left office, the use of the cabinet staff declined until it was revived by President Gerald R. Ford in the 1970s. The staff has remained active ever since.

Although he is said to have slept at times through its meetings, President Ronald W. Reagan made some further changes to strengthen the cabinet. He set up seven councils on specific topics, such as economic affairs, food and agriculture, and human resources, in which more than one department had an interest. These councils made it possible for the concerned heads of departments and members of the president's White House staff to discuss matters of common interest in detail without having to take up the time of the whole cabinet. They helped coordinate recommendations from both sets of presidential advisers. The councils were eventually reduced to two: domestic policy and economic policy. Presidents George H. W. Bush and Bill Clinton continued to use them.

Some presidents did not use cabinet meetings to seek advice, help make decisions, or delegate responsibility for governing. Usually, they were strong leaders who relied on their own judgment. President Abraham Lincoln often ignored his cabinet's advice. In one instance, when the entire cabinet opposed him, he announced, "Seven nays and one aye. The ayes have it." He made many important decisions on his own, such as the one to issue the Emancipation Proclamation, freeing the slaves.

Such strong presidents have used cabinet meetings to keep the heads of departments informed of their programs and to make sure these were carried out. Under President Franklin D. Roosevelt, in the 1930s and 1940s, cabinet meetings were discussion sessions. The president would go around the table asking officials if there was something they wanted to take up. Department heads were never consulted on important matters of government. Roosevelt also acted on his own in a number of instances. He made foreign policy and important military decisions during World War II without consulting his secretary of state or his secretaries of war and the navy. Vice President Harry S. Truman, a regular member of the cabinet, was not told about Roosevelt's plans either. This made it difficult for him to take over when Roosevelt died. In the 1960s, President John F.

☆ ══════ ☆

President Dwight D. Eisenhower's cabinet in May 1953

Kennedy, following Roosevelt's example, at times ignored his own secretary of state and made foreign policy himself. He did, however, manage to keep his vice president informed.

Other strong presidents have held cabinet meetings only to show support for their programs. In the 1960s, President Lyndon B. Johnson met with his cabinet regularly to make it appear that the heads of departments were united behind his policies. The agendas were strictly arranged in advance, and there was no genuine discussion. The meetings were used to give out information to cabinet officials and bring them up to date on foreign policy developments, such as the conduct of the Vietnam War.

Presidents' relations with their cabinets have varied over the years. Presidents are most likely to get along with their heads of departments when they share a common outlook. Dwight D. Eisenhower's cabinet was very successful because most of the members were former businesspeople whose views were similar to his. Relationships between the president and his cabinet may also be good when presidents are weak, like Calvin Coolidge, and do not try to lead. Coolidge once explained why he was so inactive. "When things are going along all right, it's a good plan to let them alone." In the White House, he worked only about four hours a day and napped in the afternoons. Weak presidents do not accomplish much and rely on their cabinet to govern for them.

Some presidents have disagreed with their heads of departments. This is likely to happen when presidents appoint members of different party factions to their cabinets. It occurs more frequently when they inherit their cabinets from a previous president. For example, John Tyler's cabinet had been chosen by President William H. Harrison, who died shortly after he took the oath of office in 1841. In that same year, President Tyler's entire cabinet resigned to protest his efforts to strengthen the states at the expense of the national government. Tyler quickly replaced his defiant heads of departments.

Usually, disagreements between presidents and inherited cabinet members are solved far less dramatically. When Harry S. Truman took over as president in 1945, after Franklin D. Roosevelt died in office, he gradually replaced some of Roosevelt's appointees. Cabinet members who did not see things Truman's way were asked to resign in favor of others Truman could trust. Such was also the case when Lyndon B. Johnson became president in 1963, after President John F. Kennedy was assassinated.

At times, presidents have to dismiss individual heads of departments. These cabinet members may be incompetent, refuse to carry out the president's wishes, or embarrass the president in some way. On the other hand, some heads of departments may wish to resign for personal reasons or because they disagree very strongly with the president's decisions on important matters. Leaving the cabinet is not always a simple matter.

SIX
LEAVING
THE CABINET

The Constitution does not say whether the president, Congress, or both may dismiss heads of executive departments. It does, however, give Congress the right to remove cabinet members who are found guilty of treason or other "high crimes and misdemeanors." No one, though, has been discharged for such wrongdoing. In the early days of the American republic, it was widely believed that the president had to get the consent of the Senate to remove officials he had appointed with Senate approval. That is why a law was introduced in Congress in 1798 to give John Adams the power to discharge Timothy Pickering, the only secretary of state to be fired by a president. Pickering had repeatedly failed to support Adams's programs.

President Andrew Jackson (1829–1837) took a different approach to the problem. He had official papers appointing cabinet officers to their posts include a statement that they served at the pleasure of the president. As a result, he could ask them to leave office whenever he wished. During his two terms, he had five secretaries of the treasury, four secretaries of state, three attorneys general, two secretaries of war, and two postmasters general.

The first of his many personnel changes took place in 1831 when Martin Van Buren, his loyal secretary of state, engineered the resignation of the entire cabinet. The members had been divided in their support of the president's controversial programs. In addition, they and their wives had deliberately snubbed Peggy Eaton, wife of Secretary of War John H. Eaton, because she was a tavern keeper's daughter. Jackson and Van Buren found their behavior toward her unacceptable. It is no wonder the president turned away from them and began to consult more often with his so-called Kitchen Cabinet.

Very few presidents have completed their terms without making changes in their cabinets. Often, they replaced individuals who did not do their jobs, defied them, or embarrassed them. Only William H. Harrison (1841), Zachary Taylor (1849–1850), Franklin Pierce (1853–1857), and James A. Garfield (1881) managed to keep all their original cabinet officers. There is a simple reason for this. With the exception of Franklin Pierce, these presidents died shortly after they took office.

By the 1860s, it had already become customary for presidents to remove heads of executive departments without consulting the Senate, but Congress was not quite prepared to admit defeat. In 1867, the lawmakers passed the Tenure of Office Act, requiring Senate approval before a cabinet officer could be dismissed. The issue came to a head when President Andrew Johnson deliberately defied the act. He fired his first secretary of war, Edward Stanton, without consulting the Senate. At the end of the Civil War, Stanton had sided with members of Congress who wanted to punish the defeated South for leaving the Union. He refused to cooperate with President Johnson, who preferred a less harsh approach. The Senate reinstated Stanton as secretary of war. His dismissal was one of the reasons Congress tried to remove Johnson from office. The lawmakers failed by only one vote. The Tenure of Office Act was never tested in the Supreme Court, but a similar 1876 law concerning postmasters was declared to be invalid by the Court in 1926. Since then, the president's right to dismiss members of the cabinet has not been seriously challenged.

Cabinet members may choose to resign their posts for personal reasons or ill health. Others leave because the president repeatedly fails to take their advice or because they cannot accept his decisions. Most are team players who leave quietly without drawing attention to themselves. For example, in 1968, Defense Secretary Robert S. McNamara withdrew from President Lyndon B. Johnson's cabinet because he disagreed with the president's plans to increase American involvement in the Vietnam War. He had stated his opinions to the president and other government officials, but he did not discuss them in public.

In 1915, however, President Woodrow Wilson's first secretary of state, William Jennings Bryan, decided to publicize the reason he had resigned. As a pacifist, opposed to war, he feared that the United States was about to be drawn into World War I. This was why he objected to Wilson's strong protests over the German sinking of the British passenger ship *Lusitania,* which

☆ ══════ ☆

This photo was taken ca. 1910 before William Jennings Bryan became secretary of state to Woodrow Wilson. He was known for his eloquent political oratory.

took 128 American lives. The United States entered the war in 1917. In response to Bryan's announcement, the newspapers accused him of disloyalty and questioned his character and motives. The careers of cabinet officers who have publicly disagreed with their presidents have often been damaged or destroyed.

On the other hand, some department officials have become heroes when it was learned why they had to leave the government. The "Saturday Night Massacre" offers a dramatic example. On Saturday, October 20, 1973, Republican president Richard M. Nixon's third attorney general, Elliot L. Richardson, and Deputy Attorney General William Ruckelshaus turned in their resignations. They had refused to obey the president's order to fire independent lawyer Archibald Cox, a special prosecutor hired solely for the purpose of investigating a sensitive problem within the government. Another member of the Department of Justice, Robert Bork, finally carried out the presidential order. Cox had demanded tapes of Nixon's conversations concerning a break-in at the Democratic Party headquarters in the Watergate apartment complex. The tapes, made during and after the 1972 presidential campaign, linked the break-in to members of Nixon's White House staff. The president refused to hand them over to Cox. Ronald Ziegler, the presidential press secretary, quickly announced to reporters that Cox had been dismissed and that Elliot L. Richardson and William Ruckelshaus had been discharged of further duties. To an angry Congress and an outraged public, it seemed clear that Nixon's unreasonable behavior had forced the three men to leave their government posts.

Other cabinet members' careers have been ruined when heads of departments were forced to resign in disgrace because they were accused of wrongdoing. Their actions resulted in scandals that embarrassed the presidents they served. Usually, these presidents were too weak to govern effectively and delegated too many responsibilities to their cabinets. They failed to supervise their cabinet officers or give them guidance and direction.

Two of the most notorious scandals in American history involved cabinet members who took bribes. William W. Belknap, one of President Ulysses S. Grant's secretaries of war, was accused of accepting illegal payments in exchange for giving certain traders the right to sell their goods on Indian reservations. The traders charged high prices for their shoddy merchandise and made enormous profits, which they shared with Belknap. In 1876, members of Congress investigated his activities and decided to remove him from office, but he resigned before they could act.

Then, in 1921 and 1922, President Warren G. Harding's secretary of the interior, Albert B. Fall, convinced Secretary of the Navy Edwin L. Denby to turn over navy oil leases at Teapot Dome in Wyoming to private developers. Fall received huge bribes from the developers for arranging this deal and one at Elk Hills in California. He resigned from the cabinet in late 1922 to enjoy his illegal gains; however, his lavish spending soon gave him away. In 1923, the scandal was discovered. Although Denby was innocent of any wrongdoing, he resigned to protect the president. In 1929, Fall became the first cabinet member to be sentenced to prison for crimes he committed while holding office. There have been many other cabinet scandals, but Teapot Dome has remained a lasting symbol of political corruption in government.

Since then, several other cabinet members have had to resign because of suspected misconduct. Among them was President Richard M. Nixon's second attorney general, Richard G. Kleindienst, who left office in 1973. He pleaded guilty to giving false testimony to the Senate concerning illegal campaign contributions from the International Telephone and Telegraph Company. He received a thirty-day suspended sentence.

Raymond J. Donovan, President Ronald W. Reagan's sec-

*Albert B. Fall, secretary of the interior in the Harding administration,
was destroyed politically by the Teapot Dome scandal.*

retary of labor from 1981 to 1985, was the first head of an
executive department to be indicted, or formally accused of
wrongdoing, while holding office. After two investigations
cleared him of ties to organized crime, he faced new charges
and resigned. A former vice president of a New Jersey construction company, he was accused of fraud in a subway project
undertaken before he joined the cabinet. After a lengthy trial, he
was found innocent of the charges brought against him.

Many honest and hardworking heads of departments have
gone on to higher office when they left the cabinet. Eight

became president of the United States. (See chart in appendix.) In the early days of the republic, it seemed as if the secretary of state was guaranteed promotion to the presidency. In the twentieth century, however, a former secretary of war, William H. Taft, and a former secretary of commerce, Herbert C. Hoover, were chosen to lead the nation. In addition, twelve cabinet members were appointed to the Supreme Court. Only five of them had been attorneys general. (See chart in appendix.) Seven were even made chief justice, the highest judge in the land.

Within the cabinet, secretaries of state have received the most attention from the public. Perhaps this is because they were so active in extending the borders of the United States and in arranging peace settlements. In the twentieth century, five have even won the prestigious Nobel Peace Prize for their efforts to end international conflicts. (See chart in appendix.) The nation's most capable secretary of state, John Quincy Adams, held office from 1817 to 1825, long before the Nobel prizes were awarded. Serving under President James Monroe, he negotiated the border between the United States and Canada with Great Britain; purchased Florida from Spain; and helped write the Monroe Doctrine, which warned European nations not to interfere in the Western Hemisphere.

There have been other outstanding secretaries of state who did not win Nobel prizes. One was Dean Acheson, who served President Harry S. Truman from 1949 to 1953. Acheson helped develop plans to halt the Soviet Union's expansion through Europe and Asia and supported the reconstruction of Europe after World War II (1939–1945). He was involved in setting up the International Bank for Reconstruction and Development and the United Nations Relief and Rehabilitation Administration. He was the co-author of the Acheson-Lillienthal Plan to control the international spread of nuclear weapons, a plan the Soviet Union rejected at that time. Acheson was also one of the architects of the North Atlantic Treaty Alliance (NATO), the first peacetime mutual defense treaty ever

☆ ══════ ☆

Dean Acheson signing the North Atlantic Treaty in April 1949,
with President Truman and Vice President Allen Barkley beside him.

signed by the United States. It requires its members to aid each
other if attacked.

Other heads of departments have made important contributions to the nation. For example, Treasury Secretary
Alexander Hamilton, who served President George Washington
from 1789 to 1795, helped strengthen the new government.
Among his achievements, Hamilton gave the United States a
sound economy. He used taxes to pay off debts that the nation
had run up during the War of Independence. He created a
national bank to manage the government's money and protect-
ed infant industries from foreign competition. Hamilton looked

forward to the day when the United States would become a major industrial power.

Herbert C. Hoover proved to be a talented organizer and manager as secretary of commerce from 1921 to 1928, under Presidents Warren G. Harding and Calvin Coolidge. He arranged for the Census Bureau to collect more data that businesses could use and encouraged his department to help companies sell their products abroad. He began the government's supervision of radio broadcasting and commercial aviation. He also asked for studies that led to the construction of Boulder (now called Hoover) Dam and later to the development of the St. Lawrence Seaway. In 1927, he organized relief for the victims of a devastating flood along the Mississippi River.

Henry L. Stimson was another dedicated public official. A Republican, he had served with distinction as secretary of war under President William H. Taft from 1911 to 1913 and as secretary of state for President Herbert C. Hoover from 1929 to 1933. He was seventy-three years old when President Franklin D. Roosevelt, a Democrat, called him back into service as secretary of war in 1940. To Stimson fell the task of preparing the United States for war, and when it came in 1941, he supervised the recruitment, training, and operations of the armed forces. He was Roosevelt's chief adviser on the atomic bomb. When Roosevelt died in 1945, the secretary of war told President Harry S. Truman about this new secret weapon and recommended that it be used against Japan. During the selection of target cities, Stimson managed to spare Kyoto, the cultural capital of Japan and the site of many art treasures. He retired in 1945.

The achievements of many other individual heads of departments have also made history, but the collective accomplishments of presidential cabinets are less likely to be remembered. After all, what goes on in cabinet meetings is not publicized. It is known that cabinet members review presidential programs, offer new ideas and constructive criticism, and occasionally make decisions about governing. Cabinet officials may make a president's plans more popular by supporting them in Congress, explaining them to the public, and carrying them out efficiently. Although presidents have increasingly turned to trusted advisers from the White House staff to help them run the government, the cabinet has not outlived its usefulness. Presidents still require advice and cooperation from their heads of departments, and the cabinet is still prepared to give it.

CABINET MEMBERS WHO LATER BECAME PRESIDENT OF THE UNITED STATES

☆

Cabinet Member	Cabinet of	Position
Thomas Jefferson	George Washington	Secretary of State
James Madison	Thomas Jefferson	Secretary of State
James Monroe	James Madison	Secretary of State and Secretary of War
John Quincy Adams	James Monroe	Secretary of State
Martin Van Buren	Andrew Jackson	Secretary of State
James Buchanan	James K. Polk	Secretary of State
William H. Taft	Theodore Roosevelt	Secretary of War
Herbert C. Hoover	Warren G. Harding and Calvin Coolidge	Secretary of Commerce

CABINET MEMBERS WHO LATER SERVED
ON THE UNITED STATES SUPREME COURT

☆

Name	Cabinet of	Position	Year
John Marshall	John Adams	Secretary of State	1801
Roger B. Taney	Andrew Jackson	Attorney General Secretary of the Treasury (acting)	1836
Nathan Clifford	James K. Polk	Attorney General	1858
Salmon P. Chase	Abraham Lincoln	Secretary of the Treasury	1864
Lucius Q. Lamar	Grover Cleveland	Secretary of the Interior	1888
William H. Taft	Theodore Roosevelt	Secretary of War	1921
James C. McReynolds	Woodrow Wilson	Attorney General	1914
Charles E. Hughes	Warren G. Harding and Calvin Coolidge	Secretary of State	1930
Harlan F. Stone	Calvin Coolidge	Attorney General	1925
Robert H. Jackson	Franklin D. Roosevelt	Attorney General	1941
Frederick M. Vinson	Harry S. Truman	Secretary of the Treasury	1953
Arthur J. Goldberg	John F. Kennedy	Secretary of Labor	1962

SECRETARIES OF STATE WHO HAVE
WON THE NOBEL PRIZE FOR PEACE
☆

Secretary	President	Reason	Year
Elihu Root	Theodore Roosevelt	for efforts to improve relations with Latin America; treaties to solve differences with European nations peacefully; settlement of Newfoundland fishing rights dispute with Great Britain	1912
Frank B. Kellogg	Calvin Coolidge	for Kellogg–Briand Pact of 1928 outlawing war	1929
Cordell Hull	Franklin D. Roosevelt	for preparing the way for the creation of the United Nations	1945
George C. Marshall	Harry S. Truman	for developing the European Recovery Program that helped nations rebuild after World War II	1953
Henry A. Kissinger	Richard M. Nixon	for negotiations to end the Vietnam War	1973

agendas schedules of topics for discussion.

Articles of Confederation the nation's first constitution, in effect from 1781 to 1788. It created an association of independent states without a national executive and did not give Congress the power to provide a common money system, raise taxes, govern the people directly, or keep the states from quarreling among themselves over trade.

bureaucracy government employees, chosen by competitive tests, who carry on the day-to-day business of government. They work for the executive departments and federal government agencies in Washington, D.C., and in branch offices throughout the nation.

cabinet in the United States, a group that advises the president, made up of the heads of executive departments, the vice president, and others the president selects to join them. In Great Britain and some other countries, the cabinet actually governs.

chief justice the head of the Supreme Court.

Congress the nation's lawmakers, who serve either in the House of Representatives for two-year terms or in the Senate for six-year terms. The number of representatives elected from each state depends on the size of its population. Each state has two senators.

Constitution a written document describing and limiting the powers of the national government. It went into effect in 1789.

departments organizations that supervise and conduct the nation's foreign affairs, agricultural and industrial programs, and so forth.

executive branch the officials who carry out the nation's laws under the direction of the president, including members of the cabinet departments.

executive privilege the president's right to withhold from the public the content of private discussions with advisers, White House memos, and other information, except under special circumstances.

factions small groups within a political party that hold common opinions or represent certain sections of the country.

Great Seal a design displaying a bald eagle clutching thirteen arrows in one talon and an olive branch in the other along with the motto *E Pluribus Unum* (Out of Many, One). It is found on all official documents and papers of the United States government.

indicted to be formally accused of misconduct.

judiciary the court system that holds trials under the law and makes sure the laws are fair.

legislature elected representatives who make the nation's laws.

minutes written records of what is said at meetings.

political party an organization that sponsors candidates for public office and helps them get elected.

president-elect refers to the victorious presidential candidate before taking the oath of office.

prime minister the title given to the head of the cabinet in Great Britain and some other countries. He or she serves as the chief executive, leader of the political party in power, and the chief lawmaker.

secretaries the titles given to heads of executive departments in the United States, Great Britain, and some other countries.

separation of powers   division of the American national government into three different parts: the legislature, to make laws; the executive branch, to carry them out; and the judiciary, to judge them.

special prosecutors   independent lawyers hired to investigate sensitive problems within the government.

Supreme Court   the highest court in the United States.

transition team   helps a new president choose heads of executive departments and other appointed officials. This team consults with the outgoing presidential staff and makes plans for taking over the executive branch.

United Nations   an organization of the world's countries.

White House staff   aides who assist the president by giving advice and information. They also help the president coordinate all the government agencies, councils, and organizations in the executive branch of government. Among the members of the White House staff are assistants to the president for national security affairs, for legislative affairs, and for policy development, in addition to a cabinet secretary and a press secretary.

Bledsoe, W. Craig. "Cabinet," *Congressional Quarterly's Guide to the Presidency,* Michael Nelson, ed. Washington, D.C.: Congressional Quarterly, n.d.: 975–985.

De Gregorio, William A. *The Complete Book of U.S. Presidents.* New York: Barricade Books, 1993.

Fenno, Richard. *The President's Cabinet.* New York: Vintage Books, 1959.

Gray, Robert K. "Some Eisenhower Impacts on the Presidential Office." Paper prepared for delivery at the annual meeting of the American Political Science Association, St. Louis, Mo., 1961.

Henderson, Philip G. "Organizing the Presidency for Effective Leadership: Lessons from the Eisenhower Years." *Presidential Studies Quarterly* 12, no. 1 (1987): 43–69.

Hoxie, R. Gordon. "Staffing the Ford and Carter Presidencies." *Presidential Studies Quarterly* 10, no. 3 (Summer 1980): 378–401.

Kirschten, Dick. "Decision Making in the White House: How Well Does It Serve the President?" *National Journal,* 3 April 1982, 584–589.

————. "Under Reagan, Power Residues with Those Who Station Themselves at His Door." *National Journal,* 25 February 1984, 361–364.

Pfiffner, James P. "White House Staff versus the Cabinet: Centripetal and Centrifugal Roles." *Presidential Studies Quarterly* 16, no. 4 (1986): n.p.

Sherrill, Robert G. "Cabinet Eaves-Dropping: Leaked Minutes." *The Nation,* 30 September 1978, 306.

Sherrill, Stephen. "Everything You Ever Wanted to Know about the Cabinet (But Found Too Boring to Ask)." *Mademoiselle* (May 1993): 154–155.

Smith, William Henry. *History of the Cabinet of the United States.* Baltimore: Industrial Printing Company, 1925.

Weisband, Edward, and Thomas M. Franck. *Resignation in Protest: Political and Ethical Choices between Loyalty to Team and Loyalty to Conscience in American Public Life.* New York: Viking Press, 1975.

White House Weekly, 3 April 1989, 5–7.

World Almanac and Book of Facts 1994. New York: Funk & Wagnalls, 1993.

World Almanac of U.S. Politics 1991–1993. New York: Pharos Books, 1991.

★ ═══ **FURTHER READING** ═══ ★

Bernotas, Bob, Jr. *The Federal Government: How It Works.* New York: Chelsea House, 1992.

Feinberg, Barbara Silberdick. *American Political Scandals: Past and Present.* New York: Franklin Watts, 1992.

Mulford, Carolyn. *Elizabeth Dole: Public Servant.* Hillside, N.J.: Enslow, 1992.

Parker, Nancy W. *The President's Cabinet and How It Grew.* New York: PLB/HarperCollins, 1991.

Sullivan, George. *How the White House Really Works.* New York: Scholastic Books, 1990.

Barbara Silberdick Feinberg graduated with honors from Wellesley College where she was elected to Phi Beta Kappa. She holds a Ph.D. in political science from Yale University. Among her more recent books are *Watergate: Scandal in the White House*, *American Political Scandals Past and Present*, *The National Government, State Governments, Local Governments, Words in the News: A Student's Dictionary of American Government and Politics, Harry S. Truman, Chief Justice John Marshall* (provisional title), *Hiroshima and Nagasaki*, and *The Wall Street Crash, October 29, 1929* (provisional title). She has also written *Marx and Marxism, The Constitution: Yesterday, Today, and Tomorrow*, and *Franklin D. Roosevelt, Gallant President*. She is a contributor to *The Young Reader's Companion to American History*.

Mrs. Feinberg lives in New York City with her sons Jeremy and Douglas and two Yorkshire terriers, Katie and Holly. Among her hobbies are growing African violets, collecting antique autographs of historical personalities, and listening to the popular music of the 1920s and 1930s.